The Perfect Pond Detective Book 2

Physical and Mechanical problems

problems

Peter J May

CONTENTS

1 Introduction 4

2 Avoiding Physical Problems 6

3 Maintenance Schedule 12

4 Troubleshooting Water Loss 14

5 Biological Filters 34

6 Pumps and Pumping 46

7 Common Chemicals 58

  Bibliography 60

  Conversion Tables 62

  Index 63

© 1998 Kingdom Books, PO Box 15, Waterlooville PO7 6BQ, England.

t.f.h.
KINGDOM

CHAPTER ONE
INTRODUCTION

A beautiful water garden has a magical atmosphere of permanence and peace. It is no wonder that the ancient Greeks felt that we shared the physical space of this focal point of a garden with the immortals who existed in the same time and space but on a different plane. Here is a place that will exist forever.

The Greeks shared their gardens with immortals.

With the materials used to construct water gardens today, this is more of a dream than a reality, even though over the last few years the quality of these materials has improved vastly. Increasingly-reassuring guarantees leap at us from the packaging on the retail outlet's shelves: liners guaranteed for 30 years, pumps continuously rated for three years, pre-formed pools and waterfall units rated for 10 years. Apart from the fact that even these extensive guarantees come to an end one day, the contingencies of market forces and competition have meant that for years manufacturers have been fighting to keep their prices down. This has meant that, although material and appliance prices are little different from what they were 10 years ago, the improvements in quality and manufacture are not what they could be, or they are not of a consistently high standard. Leaving much of what could be said unsaid, what this all means is that a modern water garden constructed from the generally-available materials will, almost inevitably, suffer trials and tribulations caused by those materials and products – and sooner rather than later.

This book shows you how to pinpoint the problems, solve them and avoid them in the future. From avoiding potential problems from the start, through a diagnosis of symptoms and an order of procedure, it shows you how most of the physical problems of the water garden are easily dealt with.

Whether you have inherited a water garden or had one built for you, or whether your water garden is your own creation and pride and joy, if you wish to keep on top of any possible problems, then this book is essential for your peace of mind. When things go wrong, perhaps from some intrusion or upset brought from the bigger, outside world, this book will guide you through the mayhem or panic and help you to sort things out in the fastest and most logical way.

Using the Book

Familiarise yourself with the contents, and see what the book has to offer. After that, it can be used as a guide to help you look for the cause of any particular problem. Sometimes I may repeat myself, but only to avoid sending you backwards and forwards in the text. Sometimes I may express myself extremely briefly because I may be touching on something covered in more detail in the companion books, *Biological Balance* or *The Perfect Pond Recipe Book*. In these cases I will refer to where the information can be gleaned in more detail.

Nowadays we share our gardens with wild life!

CHAPTER TWO
AVOIDING PHYSICAL PROBLEMS

Planting and stocking your water garden, its site and situation are covered with regard to pool health in the companion volume to this one, *Biological Balance*. However, if you are yet to embark on your water garden construction, or if your water garden always seems to have some sort of problem, consider the points below. The creation of a water garden is a building project and, like all building projects, the more effort that goes into the planning and preparation, the easier the later stages will seem. This will allow you to give free reign to your artistic flair and inspiration.

Costs in Finance and Energy

You must steer clear of some false economies. For instance, if you want to create a large pool, you need a top-quality, robust liner, and even the best liner is better preserved with a protective matting underneath as well as sand.

In fact, it would be advisable to work out exactly what your project will cost in advance, and to plan it from beginning to end. Then you can apportion sensible amounts of money to the best-quality materials and products that will give you peace of mind.

Go through every stage of the construction in your mind, budgeting the finances and estimating the energy that will be required. As the project nears completion, the actual finish seems to approach ever more slowly. It always helps to allow yourself plenty of time for a big site clear-up at the end.

Physical Considerations

Site and Situation
1. Full sun and shelter from cold and prevailing winds. This is mainly for the health of the pool and its plant life.
2. Keep away from trees, especially those with toxic leaves, such as oak, laburnum, elder and yew. Apart from the physical effort of having to clean tree leaves out of the pool more often than necessary, or having to cover the pool with a net, some trees have root growth that can undermine a pool liner or even sucker up through it. Examples are poplars, cherries and willows.
3. Avoid the boggy, waterlogged part of the garden. Water tables are pretty uncompromising things, and will just push a liner or pool up and away. Make a bog garden down there instead using a liner with holes in.

Size
This is mainly to do with the biological balance of the pool. The larger the pool, the more stable the environment seems to be. If you are contemplating having fish, then it is essential to have an absolute minimum area of 2.8 sq m (30 sq ft) and a depth of 46cm (18in). Therefore, bear this in mind when you are budgeting liner costs. Choose the best quality you can afford.

Shape
Keep the shape simple. This helps to prevent any dead spots occurring as the water circulates naturally around the pool. If you are using a liner, it also allows for maximum effective use of the liner material and, if PVC or rubber is used, there are less folds in the material.

Design and Construction

Pools

Whatever the material that you use to line your water garden, whether it is a preformed plastic, fibreglass or a flexible liner, consider whether you are likely to see any exposed material above the water level. A stream or waterfall, if you are planning such features, always take some volume of water to run them, so the level of the bottom pool drops, revealing the inside edge of the pool. If this exposes the liner, it can be obscured to a certain extent with a dense marginal planting around the edge. Also a shady overhang of 2.5–5cm (1–2in) from a rock or paving edge helps.

The reason I mention this is that any lining material exposed to the light of day (the ultra-violet rays of sunlight) is broken down to crispy flakes eventually. Although this deterioration is less rapid nowadays than it has ever been, if you are using a flexible liner you can take the opportunity of building on the inside of the pool right down to the marginal shelf or further. This obscures those upper inches of liner from sunlight forever, so the liner need never degenerate. (However, it makes changing the liner pretty difficult.)

Also, in the construction, be aware of the problems of capillary action and minute siphoning. Read the relevant chapter of this book (page 20) to familiarise yourself with the problems that can occur. A level overflow pipe set at the preferred water level will prevent some of these problems.

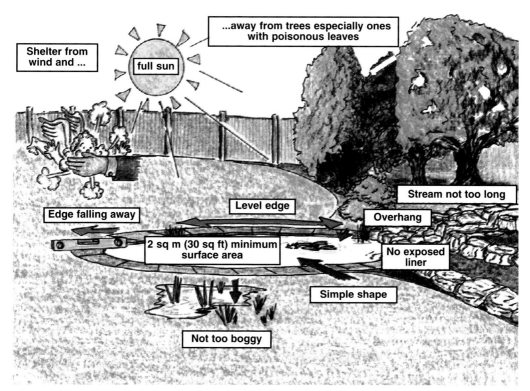

Physical considerations and design.

Streams

For the reason above (exposing the liner in the pool), beware of making streams or waterfalls disproportionately large in relation to the pool. Remember that a stream needs at least 1.25cm (0.5in) of water added to its surface to get it flowing, and this must come from the pool. Not only this, there is a backlog of water that seems to get hidden in the system. This can mean a considerable loss of water from the pool once the stream is in full flood. The marginal plants in particular cannot stand the radical rise and fall in water level.

In order to limit the demand for water from the final pool, design any waterways, streams or waterfalls so that they are effectively a series of pools running from one into another. This means that water is retained in the stream up to the level at which any fresh water pumped into the stream or stream section would immediately flow out into the next section or back into the pool.

These ideas are explained in more detail in *The Perfect Pond Recipe Book*.

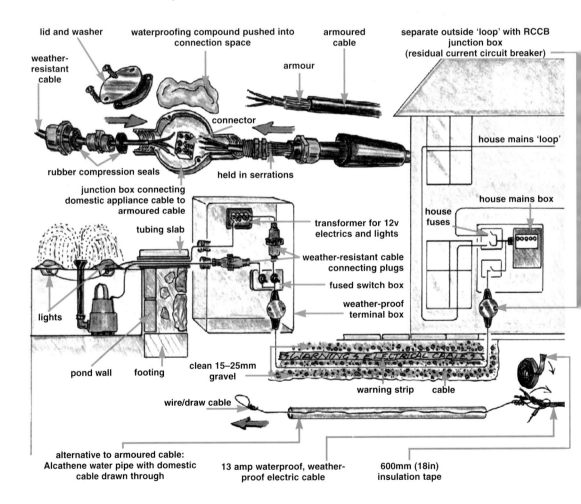

Some of the requirements and suggestions for a safe installation of a power supply to your pool.

Christmas and birthday presents are no longer a problem...

Electrics

Plan as if you were going to include all the possible accessories and features, even if it had not crossed your mind to have a pool heater, a pump for an inpool fountain, filter and filter pump, ultra/violet (u/v) lamp, waterfall, rockery lights, underwater lights and squirting frog. Even if the hobby doesn't become an addiction, friends and relatives will breathe a sigh of relief, as Christmas and birthday presents are now no longer a problem. (It's difficult to avoid. Having a pool automatically means that at some time or another you will own a squirting frog. It's like the late 60's phenomena – own a Ford Cortina and you will surely receive furry dice and a steering wheel glove.)

Therefore, get at least 13 amps worth of mains supply out there so that all this is catered for. (That is, unless you are really going to show off on the pump/white water waterfall side of things – then you should be thinking of 3-phase electricity.) The cable should be of the correct grade of armoured cable which should run, where possible, at a minimum of 46cm (18in) depth set in 15cm (6in) of gravel with a plastic warning strip laid on top. However, these specifications could change at any time, so do check them out with a qualified electrician.

Many electricians are content to run ordinary weatherproof cable through Alcathene water main pipe to protect it. If you leave 'draw cord' in the pipe, then you have the option of pulling extra wires through for additional circuits in the future. If you have run armoured cable to the poolside, then it might seem as though you are stuck with having to switch items off and on where the mains terminate. However, if the cable is 'three core', an electrician can use the 'armour' of the cable as an earth wire, two of the wires as separate 'live wires' and the remaining one as a combined 'neutral'. If you have the forethought to lay down 'four core', you have the option of creating three circuits, each of which you can control from the house.

Pool pumps, lights, u/v lamps and so on must be on an outdoor circuit, separate from the house ring main, and fitted with the latest technology in circuit breakers. Just plugging them into the back of an old lawnmower RCD on the house ring main is totally inadequate. If you can afford it, have a separate circuit breaker for each item, or at least keep lighting separate from everything else, as this tends to be the most temperamental item with regard to earth leakages.

I must stress further that all electrics and electrical items need to be installed to the correct National Standards. Have them installed, or at least checked, by a fully-qualified electrician.

Pumps and Pumping

Many a glass of beer has been diluted by tears caused by the behaviour, breakdown and misinformation about pumps. There ought to be a publicised league table of the reliability of pumps, because I now believe that no new pump brought out on the market, especially if it is an 'improvement' on preceding models, seems to outlast or outperform any that has gone before. If this notion turns out to be a complete fallacy, then thank goodness!

Most of the pumps produced for domestic consumption are marketed in a cut-throat world of heavy competition and, therefore, extreme economic stringencies. As a result, you get what you pay for. For real durability and maintainability, you need to pay three times as much as they ask for the sort of products that are available from retail outlets.

Choose a pump for:
(a) its reliability – is it continuously rated?
(b) its availability locally from a retailer you like and get on with.
(c) its performance. This includes its suitability for its purpose. You do not want a pump that needs the protection of a thick foam prefilter if it is meant to be supplying water to a filter system.

For more detail on the types of pump, see *Pumps and Pumping*, Chapter 6.

Filters and Filtration

For every pond there is a specific size of filter that needs a specific size of pump to recycle the water through it. Some manufacturers, using more sophisticated filter media and with ancillary accoutrements and 'add-ons' such as ultra-violet lamps and magnets, have reduced the size theoretically necessary to keep ponds of specific volumes clear, but they stick to some of the old rules for pond filtration.

1. The pond must be at least 0.5m (18in) deep.

2. The filter itself must be capable of processing half the volume of the pool every hour of the day and night.

3. Therefore there must be a pump that is capable of delivering this.

Possible results of over-specification!

Example: A 500-gallon pond needs a filter that is related to that gallonage, together with a pump that can deliver 250 gallons to the height at which the filter is sitting. Situate the pump on the opposite side of the pond to the filter inlet for efficiency.

Over-specification is better than under-specification, within reason. If the filter is churning over more than the *total* volume of the pool every hour, then the resulting commotion underwater can only be harmful to the fish.

4. It used to be necessary to have a filter surface area that was one third of the pool surface area. Modern manufacturers producing compact multistage units claim otherwise. It is useful to bear this in mind since a manufacturer's claim to guaranteeing water *clarity* does not guarantee the *quality* of that water. After all, water containing ammonia and nitrites can still be quite clear.

5. The water must be well oxygenated by waterfall, fountain or plants.

Note
Total volume of your pond in gallons = length in feet x breadth in feet x depth in feet x 6.25.

CHAPTER THREE
MAINTENANCE SCHEDULE

The main ingredient of success in good water garden management is to have a diligent eye. If you make a point of taking a good look at how your water garden is progressing week by week, then you will be aware of any changes that may require some remedial action.

During any extremes of temperature, be particularly watchful. Also, take a look after any stormy weather. Plants can easily be bowled over in their baskets.

General Maintenance

Weekly in Spring, Summer and Autumn
- Check pumps and clear prefilters.
- Check u/v lamps and sterilizer units (see u/v lamps, page 44).
- Check the filter. Does it smell right? Rinse settlement chamber brushes in pond or rain water if necessary.
- Clear fountain nozzles and debris from waterfalls as necessary.

Monthly in Spring, Summer and Autumn
- Back flush struggling biological filters if the facility is available or clear out the worst of the sludge.

Every Six Months
- Change u/v lamp bulb and carefully clean the quartz sleeve.
- Filters struggling with high fish populations will need a proper clean-out. Rinse the medium in pond water or rain water. *Never* use tap water. Do this when the water temperature is warm enough for biological activity, that is, when it is above 10°C (50°F). Alternatively, one of the clean-outs can be carried out at the winter close down (see below).

Winter Maintenance

Pumps
In summer, the warmer, less dense water is at the surface. As the temperature of the water drops to around 4°C (35°F), its density changes and the water that is closest to freezing becomes the least dense and floats to the top. The water at the bottom stays at a fairly steady temperature under a blanket of colder water that may freeze. Therefore, if you wish to run a submersible pump, perhaps for a biological filter, as it gets colder reduce its flow and bring it closer to the surface so that only the top 22–30cm (9–12in) of water in the pool are circulated. The depths of the pool will remain at an even temperature by being left undisturbed.

Many people recommend that in the depths of winter you should remove the pump from the pool and bring it indoors. This would certainly give you the chance to service it and clean the impellor. On induction drive motors, the smooth plate of the motor housing can be carefully cleaned with a plastic scourer.

Filters

For running filter pumps as the weather becomes cooler, see *Pumps* above.

If the temperature drops to a level at which the filter is liable to freeze up, turn it off, drain it and rinse out the medium with pond water or rain water.

If, for any reason, you have had to turn off your filter for more than a few hours, always clean it out before you turn it on.

Spring Maintenance

Electrical Connections

Dampness and moisture will always build up, even in the most weather-resistant cable connectors, resulting in circuit breakers tripping unaccountably. Check the inside of lamps, too. Try greasing seals with vaseline, but do not be surprised at the moisture build up simply as a result of the humidity in the atmosphere.

Tubing

Algae which has built up in lengths of tubing exposed to sunlight the previous summer often needs to be flushed out.

Filters

As the weather warms up, make sure the filter has been thoroughly cleaned before it needs to be brought into action.

If the weather is sunny from very early on in the season, then the filter will have plenty of work, as algae growth takes advantage of the situation before the water plants and oxygenators get into gear. Therefore, check it regularly.

Summer Maintenance

See *Weekly Routine*, above. Keep checking, especially in sultry, humid weather.

Autumn Maintenance

Keep the pond clear of falling leaves, covering it with a net if necessary. Sheltered, non-conservation type ponds can be tidied up around the marginal areas. Cut back plants that have died back. Otherwise, leave this until the spring as cover for amphibians and some frost protection for emergent growth.

For More Help

For a more complete guide to maintenance, see *The Perfect Pond Detective Book 1: The Biological Balance*.

TROUBLESHOOTING WATER LOSS

If the pool is losing water, you must follow a process of elimination. Don't panic.

Process of Elimination

More often than not, water loss is not a case of SOS flares, sirens, bells and 'all hands to the pumps'. It is more a matter of a definite disappearance of the odd inch or two – in some cases, intermittently. The result is that you find you are regularly topping up with tap water which feeds algae and irritates the fish, so you end up with green water and sickly fish you cannot see, or spend a fortune on chemicals to 'condition' the water.

Evaporation

If it is a hot summer and the water loss is little more than an inch or two a week, the cause could very easily be evaporation. This is even more apparent when you have a new pool with, perhaps, a rock edge of fairly water-absorbent stone that actually sits in the water. Some stone can act as quite an efficient wick for evaporation. A new, unsealed, unpainted fountain ornament can have the same effect.

Cure: If the cause is evaporation by wick effect, then this generally cures itself as a 'verdigris' of algae and moss builds up on the stone. In my part of the world, pond-keepers speed up the process of weathering by painting on a foul concoction of milk, cow muck and honey ... mmmm.

Fountain ornaments that suck up the water can be sealed with a stone sealant or matt G4 epoxy varnish.

Liner Leaks

This includes concrete. Do you lose water when the filter, waterfalls or fountain are running? If you don't know, try leaving it for a while with everything switched off and the pool just standing. If the water level still drops, it is the liner. Don't despair. The cure is easy – it is the cause that can be the mystery.

Whilst keeping a careful eye on the situation, see what level the water will sink to. It may be that the damage is restricted to the upper regions and the water level sinks to the level of the hole in the liner. In this case, it may be possible to effect a repair without a total clean out and 'dry out'.

Causes: Finding the cause is to begin to eliminate the problem in the future. It may be just one of the causes listed below, or a combination of more than one.

Liner age: All materials used for lining pools have a limited life expectancy. Apart from concrete, all the materials, whether rubber or plastic, flexible or rigid, are affected by the ultra-violet rays in sunlight. Present technology is improving the material's ability to withstand this ageing process, but eventually most liner materials, particularly in exposed areas at and above the water level, begin to crack up. That is the first place to look.

Things falling in, particularly rocks and animals: Look for rocks on the edge that might have tumbled in. Animals trying to get out may have caused the problem. Has your Labrador scrabbled on the side as it tried to claw its way out? Or, as it emerged in a soggy mess, did it dislodge a rock that toppled to the bottom? You rush forward in a panic just in time to get hit in the face by the obnoxious spray from a good shake.

Children love things that make a **big** splash.

Wild life: Herons can accidentally stab holes in liners. Geese and, sometimes, ducks, can do terrible things to cheap, thin liner material. Moles and mice can sometimes be inquisitive enough to investigate the edibility of this strange ballooning material that appears in their newly-excavated burrows.

Clues: If a hole in the liner does not make itself apparent after the water level has dropped to the level of the leak, the pool must be cleaned out and the liner washed down thoroughly.

First check the welded seams of the liner material. This is generally the 'Achilles heel' of newly-installed liners where there is no obvious cause of puncture.

Many liner materials weld at extremely specific temperatures. It is possible that some manufacturers, in the hot pursuit of deadlines for stocking orders, may not have been diligent enough in checking that the welding equipment is up to the correct temperature before starting the day. Also, in the early season rush, quality control seems to become an ideal rather than a reality. I would always recommend checking every inch of your liner's joins before you install it.

Clever remote top-up systems, bottom drains and bottom-fed filter systems where they meet and clamp onto liners are all areas to be suspicious of when the pool is full. When you consider that a mere 200 gallons of water weighs nearly a ton, then any sort of 'add on' to a pool liner is going to test out inadequacies in the installation once the pond is full.

If by the time you have washed down and cleaned out the pool, no holes have made themselves apparent, you must dry out the pool. During the mopping-up stage, you are bound to find pinprick holes when the water that has leaked out returns back through the holes. If you have used sand as an underlay to the liner, that will taint the water where it comes back through the holes. The holes are generally at a very exposed point, or at the centre of an indentation caused by a heavy object falling into the pool.

Don't be satisfied with the discovery of just one hole, particularly if it is small and the leak is substantial. Search diligently and methodically over the whole liner surface.

Still no holes? Check the folds, particularly in the corners of very formally-shaped pools, as these are sometimes not efficiently executed, particularly when a liner is used that might only just be the right size. Also, there can evolve a certain amount of capillary action (see page 20) in the corners, and minute siphons can get set up.

Cure: The soil surrounding the pool must be separate from the pool. This also applies to any soil in the pool that is in a marginal trough or a bog garden.

When I build a pool, it has a skeleton of concrete blocks and the liner finishes on top of these. Without this skeleton, the liner must come to the surface of the soil and be kinked so that it is upright to prevent any siphoning. Some landscapers dip the liner into a small trench and the liner is held upright and in place with a thin snake of cement or concrete lying on top of it. The top edge of the liner is then disguised with a mulch of bark, gravel or pebbles; alternatively, slabs or rock provide a definite edge, and the liner comes up behind these.

Underlay on top of the liner must not reach further than the liner.

To prevent any further possibility of siphoning, an overflow must be arranged at the maximum desired water level. Alternatively, drill holes in pointing under slabs and at the top of stonework to relieve the suction that is causing the siphoning action.

Capillary Action

Capillary action, or minute siphoning, is something that can develop at any point and be permanent or intermittent. You find the effect in liner ponds where a bog or soil comes down into the pool water, or where folds of a liner go over and down behind the sides of the pool. You might find that a temporary siphon sets itself up just after heavy rain and lasts until the water table drops sufficiently to dry it out, or it may be that the problem gets worse when the water table in the surrounding ground is low.

If the electrical cable for the pump, light, and so on, is placed over the liner, perhaps under a slab or stone through a conduit of tubing, this can easily set itself up as a siphon, particularly after heavy rain or if the pond has been over-filled. Once the water level in the pool reaches the level at which the tube comes into the pond, then the pool will siphon out through the tube to the level at which one end of the tube finishes. This effect can also set itself up in the cement behind walling or stonework.

If you have a 'natural' style of pool with a liner covered with soil but protected by a layer of underlay, you might find quite rapid siphoning occurring if the underlay lies over the edge of the pool.

Cure or Repair of Liners

Butyl or **rubber** are the easiest materials to repair, with patches that you simply push and squash into place. Alternatively, a bicycle puncture repair outfit is just as satisfactory. The liner must be very dry. Use a hair drier.

Polyethelene or **PVC** liners are repaired with proprietary PVC Repair Kits, generally available from water garden centres and swimming pool retailers. Some of these kits will work even underwater, but consider them only as emergency temporary repairs.

Fibreglass and **rigid** plastic pools can be repaired with normal fibreglass resin and matting. A typical car body repair kit contains enough materials to repair a riot of vandalism or years of accidents and decay. Some retailers used to sell an excellent ready-mixed version in a tube, but I believe that its limited shelf life put stockists off. It was particularly good for building up the edges of badly-designed and sloppily-manufactured preformed waterfall sections (see below).

ABS plastic pools can be repaired with the solvent glue for ABS drainpipes and guttering using a patch made from an offcut of the same plastic. Alternatively, use a fibreglass repair kit.

HDP plastic pools can be repaired with a fibreglass repair kit or an HDP or Butyl repair kit. However, only something really drastic can puncture one of these.

Handy Hint

For cleaning out ponds that have **flexible** or **rigid** liners: the last few gallons which a pump or siphon cannot suck down to and which are too much for a sponge or cloth can be effectively swept up with a plastic dustpan and soft brush.

Concrete Pond Leaks

These are very often a sign of the beginning of the end. If the pool is cracked, then it is either because the concrete and foundations have moved (which means that the design or construction had limitations), or the concrete has decayed because of age or bad mixing and materials. If the problem seems to be caused by movement of the concrete, then you can either go with it or stop it.

Going with it can be considered only a temporary plan of action. Chase out the cracks as deep as they go to good solid concrete and to at least 25mm (1in) width at the top. Then fill them with a thick tar or bitumen mastic. This will give you the flexibility you will need if there are any more slight movements.

Alternatively, you can fill the cracks with a mix of cement containing bonding solution. Paint the chased-out cracks with bonding solution as well. It helps to mix in a small amount of fibre, normally used for strengthening concrete.

Having said all that, this will not necessarily last five minutes if the overall structure of the pool is weak.

If, for instance, the pool is on a steep slope, there is a tremendous propensity for the thing to slide down the hill. Even if this is just a fraction of an inch a year, the result is a tremendous strain on the front edge and base of the pool. In this case, the pool must be strengthened so that it remains rigid and stable in the circumstances that it is in, or be lined with a flexible liner. This would be the sound advice given by most water garden product retailers.

Alternatively, the strengthening can come from blockwork either inside the pool and backfilled with concrete, or concrete collars poured around the outside with an additional fibre-reinforced concrete base. The thickness of this would depend on the state of the existing base, but it should be a minimum of 5cm (2in) and preferably a good 10cm (4in) deep.

If this all seems like too much upheaval, and the concrete in the pond seems to be fairly stable and perhaps only the surface is crazed, then a new 'high performance' surface render will give it the necessary extra life. A product called Fibrocem, which is a ready-mixed sand and cement, also contains fibreglass fibres stabilised chemically so that they will not dissolve in the cement. If the instructions for its application are followed precisely and it is applied to clean, stable concrete, it can be very efficient and is more durable against accidental damage than any flexible liner – but it works out twice as expensive as the most expensive liners.

Very fine hair-line cracks in concrete can be stabilised by various paints. Products designed for the building industry to waterproof water containers or tank buildings can be effective, but check for pollutants (chlorines and algicides are in exterior paints) and also excessive lime. Bitumen paint is a good standby if you don't mind black.

The rubber paints generally available to seal concrete ponds need the 'luck of the Irish' to be reliable. They need perfect humidity and a stable temperature within the right range whilst they are being applied, which seem to make them impractical.

One product that is fairly easy to obtain and that waterproofs anything that absorbs water is G4. It is an expoxy-based paint or varnish which, although a bit expensive, is most effective on wood, stone and concrete, and is the answer to many insoluble problems. You can even paint it on concrete when the surface is damp.

An alternative to flexible liners is to fibreglass the concrete. Usually this is the sort of decision taken by those who are familiar with the idiosyncrasies of the medium and probably have access to large quantities at wholesale prices. Otherwise, it is a fairly expensive and time-consuming option, but the results in proficient hands are durable and bring easy maintenance out of virtual dereliction and decay.

Clay or **puddled** ponds can crack if the weather has been dry and the sun has had a chance to bake the clay liner. As the water leaks, the sun chases the cracks further down.

To cure without putting in a flexible liner, soak the clay thoroughly and run a thumper, or plate compactor for larger areas, over it. Then just hope for the best.

I always feel that a puddled pond's guarantee of survival is to have a constant feed of fresh water from a spring or stream. This can top it up and then overflow back into its usual course (see also *Conservation Ponds,* page 30).

Filter Leaks

If there is a substantial water loss and you have an external biological filter, it is best to check this out first because you want to preserve its effectiveness for biological filtration. It is not desirable to turn the thing off for a long period whilst you check everything else.

A fine spray blowing in the face whilst standing upwind from the fountain.

If you haven't checked it for ages, you have no idea what might be lurking in there!

Clues to (left) a fountain leak and (right) a filter leak.

Clues: (a) If your biological filter has had little maintenance recently, and we are in the throes of a long hot summer, then this could be the culprit for substantial water loss. As the filter box is continually being fed with ever more grimy water; as the cycle of life in the pool increases in speed; as the water warms up, there comes a point when the bacteria are unable to cope with the breakdown of all this organic matter. The detritus begins to build up. Eventually, whatever medium is being used for filtration clogs up to the extent that it overflows. Look for drips out from under the lid (see also *Filter Problems,* page 41).

(Note: Bear this in mind before you go on a long summer holiday. If you feel that this is something that might happen at any moment whilst you are away, see *NB, Ensured Water Level,* page 30.)

(b) If there seem to be drips from under the edge of the lid and you have just cleaned out the filter and the pump, then the fresh force and vigour of the newly-cleaned system is sending the spray every which way under the filter lid. Therefore, either turn down the pump's supply of water with a gate valve, or somehow baffle the spray so that it gets knocked down into the filter without rebounding everywhere.

(c) Filters have other inherent problems. Often they are cobbled together out of materials and products that were designed for other purposes. Therefore, you have a mixture of incompatible materials held together by other materials that behave differently as temperatures rise and fall. In the cold, hose tails become brittle and crack; in the heat, jubilee clips expand and the hose becomes soft. What was a tight fit between ABS plastic and HDP now lets water flood through. Check all the fittings, especially at the inlets and outlets.

(d) Water from the main outlet can defy all the normal laws of gravity. Water that should be efficiently deposited from a wide 40mm (1.5in) tube back into the pool will drip back up the tube towards the filter on the outside even if it seems to be sloping down from the filter. It will then dribble down the side of the filter and away from the pool.

Cures: To stop water dripping back up the tube, fix an elastic band or a tight 'O' ring around the end of the outlet pipe.

With fittings, flanges and threads and hose tail threads, where appropriate use plenty of plumber's PTFE tape. Some plumbers nowadays use silicone bath sealant.

Where hoses push onto hose tails and on jubilee threads use lashings of vaseline or waterproof grease. In addition, it will help you get them undone for maintenance purposes.

Flanges could be sealed with grease, and the rubber washers that came with the fitting and are now lost can be copied using butyl or rubber liner samples from your local water garden centre. Alternatively, cut up an old hot water bottle.

Fountain Leaks

If the fountain seems to be the culprit, that is, the drop in water level ceases when the fountain is turned off, then keep it turned off in windy weather, turned down or get a more suitable fountain.

Clues: Obvious clues are damp patches on the pool edging and fountain spray in the face when standing upwind of the fountain. Fine 'sprinkly' types of fountains and bell or mushroom fountains are the most easily affected, but a very high jet or fall from an ornament is just as susceptible. Also, just because the fountain seems to be protected from the wind on all four sides in a courtyard-style setting does not mean that peculiar eddies cannot be created around buildings and over walls where the wind speed is accelerated far beyond the gentle puffs of the open environment. These may be short-lived but can occur regularly.

If the pool is small and contains a large fountain ornament, then evaporation may be the cause of the water loss (see *Evaporation*, page 18).

Cures: A fountain may need to be left on in order to oxygenate an over-populated pool. An emergency remedy is to remove the existing fountain jet so that the water emerges straight from the regulator on the submersible pump just below water level. This will

Potential leak points from filter box or ultra violet lamp

Your filter and pump should be capable of processing half the volume of your pool every hour.

For changes in weather and temperature: Jubilee clips on the hose can be maintained and tightened when greased with waterproof grease or vaseline. Grease on the hose tails will help the seal and removal.

Thread on hose tails can be sealed with plumber's PTFE tape or Hermatite.

filter box lid

brush chamber

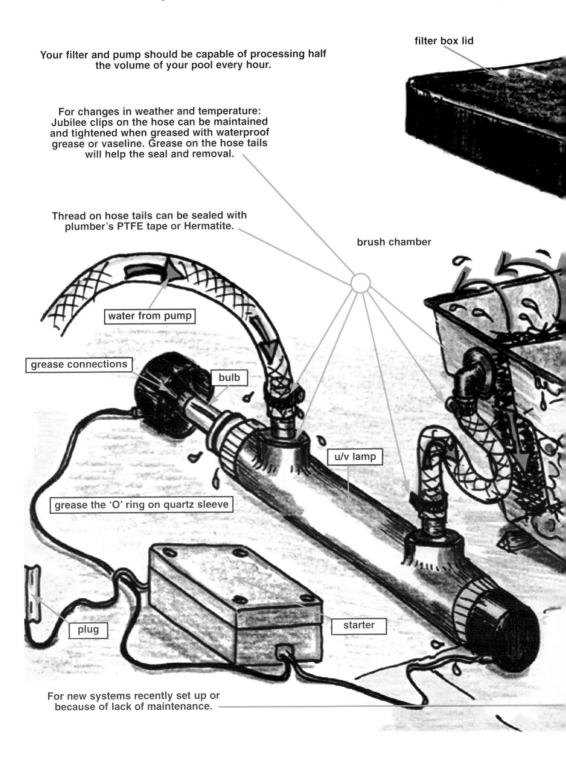

water from pump

grease connections

bulb

u/v lamp

grease the 'O' ring on quartz sleeve

plug

starter

For new systems recently set up or because of lack of maintenance.

Check a new filter system every day for the first two weeks or until it is running properly as a biological filter.

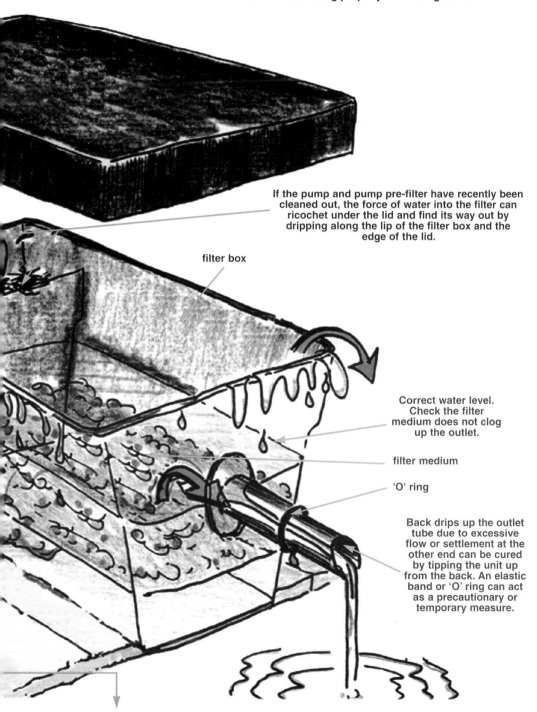

If the pump and pump pre-filter have recently been cleaned out, the force of water into the filter can ricochet under the lid and find its way out by dripping along the lip of the filter box and the edge of the lid.

filter box

Correct water level. Check the filter medium does not clog up the outlet.

filter medium

'O' ring

Back drips up the outlet tube due to excessive flow or settlement at the other end can be cured by tipping the unit up from the back. An elastic band or 'O' ring can act as a precautionary or temporary measure.

Significant backlog of sediment will eventually cause total blockage and resulting overflow.

create a certain amount of gushing effect that will mix in a bit of air with the water as the stream of water breaks the water surface producing quite effective oxygenation.

Next, think about obtaining a jet for your pump that is less affected by wind. Get wider holes in the jet or consider a gushing foam jet. With the latter, as the moving water passes through the jet, it sucks in air through holes in the body of the jet. This makes the water white and looks, supposedly, like a natural geyser.

Waterfalls

If the waterfall seems to be the problem, that is, the water level radically drops only whilst it is running, then your problems may only have just begun.

Possibilities to be eliminated: It must be remembered that for every stream, a certain amount of water must be taken from the pool to get it running. Depending on the size of the stream and the power of the pump, there will be a big loss in level from the pool. Long streams need big pools.

I calculate the loss by taking a rough approximation of the stream surface area and multiplying it by 1cm (0.5in) and adding on 10% for loss in the system. However, if you know the amount of water your pump delivered to the head of your waterfall in terms of gallon buckets full per minute, then you can calculate the amount of water loss caused by timing how long it takes from the moment you switch on to the moment water appears to be falling back into the pond. Some ponds, including one that I was involved with at the Chelsea Flower Show, can be half empty by the time that starts happening. If you top up the pool whilst it is running, then you must realise that all that same volume of water is going to overflow when you turn off at the end of the day.

Some water seems to get lost in the system as well. Each section of waterfall has a certain amount of 'backup' contained within it and the supply pipe tubing can hold quite a bit. In metric terms, 1 metre of 3.8cm tubing can hold 1.1 litre of water (in imperial measures, 1yd of 1.5in tubing can hold 2 pints of water).

Eliminating the possibilities: If it were possible to maintain the water level all the way through the stream, or series of waterfalls at the level of flowing, this would minimise the amount of water necessary to get that stream or waterfall flowing. This might seem impossible without resorting to starting again after reading *The Perfect Pond Recipe Book*, but a small improvement can be made if you place the outlet from the pump at the top header pool above the water level. This prevents the header pool siphoning dry every time you turn off the pump.

Clues: Once you have deduced that neither evaporation on the stream stonework nor water 'hiding' in the system is relevant to your problem, then we must continue the process of elimination.

A stream or waterfall flowing through the freshly made-up ground from the excavations of a newly-constructed pond has potential for problems. Freshly excavated soil doubles in volume on excavation and it will gradually shrink to the size it was in the ground. If your stream depends upon it for support you will find it tipping 'backwards' as time goes on.

Pump oxygenating a pool when a fountain jet has been removed.

Water flow emerging from just below the surface drags air into the water.

Potential points at which you may lose water on a preformed waterfall when the unit was tilted back, bent or was badly cut from the raw material.

NB With streams supplied with water from a submersible pump, it is rarely the pipework at fault. After changes in weather the plumbing to external pumps can suffer considerable stress.

1 Check the inlet hose is not leaking backwards. Also check that it is not siphoning the water back down to the pump.

2 Run the system and, as the water builds up, watch for stray rivulets, seepages sideways and upwards, particularly where the stream liner meets the pool liner.

3 Leave the stream or waterfall pool to stand and suspect any areas that lose their water entirely.

Cure: relieve the pressure.

4 Is the underlay on top of the liner to protect it? If it is one continuous strip, it will siphon the stream dry.

5 This is more easily deduced during dry weather. Look under edging stones and capping stones.

6 No joy? Take it apart and reconstruct!

Finding leaks in streams and waterfalls lined with flexible liners.

Preformed Plastic and Fibreglass Waterfalls
Check around the lips of the individual units and make sure there is no water travelling back to the soil along the edges.

Check there is no water overflowing over the back of the unit. This is a particular problem with very flexible, plastic waterfall sections. As the soil beneath consolidates or an ingress of rainwater below the units washes away the sand bed the units rest on, then the support for the units is undermined and they tip and crumple. As they do this, the problem is exacerbated as water spills out, undermining the units even more.

Cures: Many of the mass-produced waterfall and stream units are not finished as well as they might be and sometimes the odd unit is not cut precisely from the raw material. This is no real problem since there is usually too much material left on the shape rather than too much cut away.

1. Check the inlet pipe at the head of the streams. Backward drips can be a problem.
2. Check that the water is not flowing from the units properly because they are badly positioned or that they have moved.

If they have moved, nestle them back into their beds with more support from the back. Sand can be washed away easily and soil can sink or be eroded by ants. Well-placed rocks lend more dependable support.

Try to gain some more permanent support from a foundation of stone and nestle the unit in a bed of semi-dry cement and sand or mortar mix. Make sure that there are strategic barriers of rock and stone to prevent the new bed from washing into the pool before it has 'gone off'.

3. If the water still runs backwards towards the rockery despite repositioning, then it is time for the knife or hacksaw. Cut away a bit of the unit at a time until the water flows forward. (When using a sharp knife, like a Stanley knife, always cut away from you.)
4. If you still cannot find the fault, check the hose from pump to inlet. Some bright spark might have put a fork or spade through it. In all my years of water gardening, I have only known this happen once, and I was the one who did it.

Waterfalls and Streams Lined with Rubber or PVC
The process of elimination must continue to find where the leak is occurring.
1. Run the stream and waterfalls. In which part of the stream is the leak occurring?
2. Wait until all the sections of the stream and waterfall are full of water and it is ready to flow. If they were well-constructed then to a certain extent water should be held all the way down the stream. If a liner of underlay was put on top of the liner to protect it from the rockwork sitting on it, then the water will siphon down to the bottom and into the pool through the underlay. Let us hope that it isn't siphoning anywhere else.
3. Leave the stream or waterfall pools to stand and suspect those areas that lose their water entirely.
4. If there is no perceptible or unexplained loss over a few hours, try running the stream and watch for stray rivulets as the water builds up. Some setups take a while for the full force of the water to build up. If there is nothing obvious in the way of leaks or splashes, then this might need further investigation during a very dry spell.

5. One place that needs a very careful examination is where the stream liner comes down to the pool level. Is there any chance that water is being forced back up between the liners? It is also here and at other waterfalls that water can travel considerable distances sideways and even upwards behind stonework.

6. During a dry spell, check for signs of dampness and seepage. If you do find some you can probably trace it back to a place where the water is pushed out between stone and cement and liner. Water forcing down behind stonework on a waterfall can sometimes find nowhere else to go apart from up. 'Weep holes' to reduce the pressure should have been inserted (see *Seepages* below).

7. Still no dampness? There may be a hole in the liner underneath the face of a waterfall caused by a knock during construction. If there is no visible leak in the liner whether or not water is flowing, then suspect animal interference. Let's face it, you have created a perfect environment for many hole-burrowing animals and, if anything, your waterfall intrudes on their potential home. They must think it a small recompense to borrow a little of the rubber you have draped over their hillside to bulk up their nesting material.

Cure: So now the investigations get to the serious 'take it apart and have a look' or 'knock it down and start again' stages!

Read *The Perfect Pond Recipe Book* to put it back together. If there are shortfalls in the techniques of construction, now is the opportunity to get it right. If there are holes to be discovered it is the only way you will get to them. Therefore, start at the most suspicious areas and work up and then down. However, if there are no clues, start on the easy bits.

Try the cure for seepages and pressure first, just in case.

Seepages

One would think that if you have water flowing down a channel and confined by the sides of that channel it would be contained. However, when you have two layers, one of which the water both flows over and under, then some new rules come into force. In order to stop water getting pushed up the sides by the water coming up forcefully from behind, you must create holes in the upper level, that is, the stonework, to relieve the pressure. Let it flow.

When you create a stream or waterfall on top of a waterproof membrane, the temptation is to glue everything down with cement and backfill with cement behind all the facing stones. This works excellently to begin with as the cement excludes any water from travelling under the stonework. As time goes by, however, the cement relinquishes its grip on the liner and allows a thin smear of water to travel between it and the stone. This is when the problems start.

I have found that the most successful waterfalls and streams I have built have used as little cement as possible. Confine yourself to cementing in only the sill stone, and you can backfill behind the rest with round, smooth pea gravel. This, together with the very slow-moving water underneath the stone, fills in the gaps and displaces the faster-moving water that then is forced to run over the top.

If you build your streams and waterfalls with stones placed in self-supporting positions, there will never be too much upheaval even if major repairs are required in the future.

Brick faces to 'mirror-style' waterfalls can have small 'weep holes' provided by copper or plastic tubes placed in the pointing of the brickwork at the bottom of the waterfall. These drain away the water at the face of the liner.

If and when you discover a hole in the liner, then the repair is the easy part (refer to *Cure or Repair of Liners* in *Leaking Liners*, page 20). The jigsaw of replacing the stonework is a challenge but, once done, it is a satisfying achievement. A photograph can be a 'memory jogger' to help when replacing the larger stones in their original positions. For those of you fortunate enough to possess a camcorder, you could film yourself dismantling it and run the tape backwards to see how it goes back together!

Undiscoverable leaks in streams can be the bane of your life, and all other pool problems can pale into insignificance in comparison. But intermittent water loss is sometimes easier to explain.

I once met a golden retriever that drank copious quantities of water from her master's stream when it was running. When it was very hot she would lie in the bottom letting the flow wash over her as she blocked it up and it spilt over into the rockery and the rest of the garden. Large quantities of fallen leaves can have the same effect, so in the autumn consider netting the stream as well as the pool; or turn it off.

Ensured Water Level

What should you do if your filter clogs up or your fountain or waterfall suddenly starts to distribute the liquid contents of the pool over the rest of the garden leaving your plants high and dry and your fish floundering in half an inch of water? Read on:

The pump that provides any water supply to any of these items should sit in a high-sided bucket at its normal level in the pond, that is, the thickness of a brick off the bottom. In this way, if a potential disaster were to begin, when the water level sinks below the level of the sides of the bucket then the pump would run dry. This may burn out the pump, although many good pumps would only temporarily seize, or trip the RCD installed for your outside electrics. (If you haven't got one, get one.)

If the pump does burn out, this is the opportunity to get one with a float switch attached. This will turn off the pump automatically long before the water level gets dangerously low.

Alternatively, you can install a mechanical or electronic water level detection device. These can only be relied upon in clean, undisturbed environments, for example, in isolated sumps that are linked to the pool. I have seen pools linked with electronic 'top-up' devices with disastrous consequences. if you want to overcome any water level problems with any 'top-up' devices, make them purely mechanical, accessible and easy to maintain. They must have a non-return valve installed before the outlet that prevents any reverse back flow of contaminated water back up the pipework – easily obtainable from all builders' merchants and easy to plumb in.

Remember, however, 'topping up' makes your water green.

Water Loss in Conservation-style Ponds

Puddled Ponds without a Rubber or Plastic Liner under the Clay

As the summer temperatures evaporate the contents of the pond, the water level drops, exposing the clay liner. As this dries out, it starts to crack. This allows even more water to escape. Eventually the condition worsens at an ever-increasing rate as the water level chases the cracks down the sides of the pool.

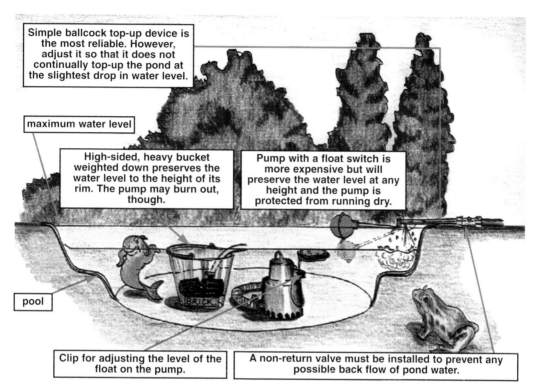

Simple ballcock top-up device is the most reliable. However, adjust it so that it does not continually top-up the pond at the slightest drop in water level.

maximum water level

High-sided, heavy bucket weighted down preserves the water level to the height of its rim. The pump may burn out, though.

Pump with a float switch is more expensive but will preserve the water level at any height and the pump is protected from running dry.

pool

Clip for adjusting the level of the float on the pump.

A non-return valve must be installed to prevent any possible back flow of pond water.

Ensured water level.

Prevention: A good, solid marginal planting will help to prevent this. As the water level of the pond drops, at least for the first few inches, only more of the marginal plants will be exposed and not the clay liner.

A good marginal planting of vigorous types can lead to another problem when deeply penetrating roots find their way through the clay puddling. Some reeds and rushes take such hold on the clay liner that they are impossible to shift without doing some damage to the clay liner. Limitation can be ensured by choosing varieties that are not so invasive of the bank (see *Perfect Pond Detective Book 1 The Biological Balance: Conservation Pools: – Choice of Plants*). If you are unfamiliar with the plant, try to find out what a mature clump should look like.

The puddling should be consistently 15cm (6in) thick from top to bottom

Repair: Once the cause of the leak or seepage is identified and removed or prevented then the area can be re-puddled with a hand-held 'thumper' of the type used by road men to consolidate small areas of scalpings or footings. For larger areas, a plate compactor raised and lowered by ropes in the pond, up and down, may be the solution.

Ponds with a Rubber or Plastic Liner
Beneath a Layer of Soil

With this style of pond construction, it is not so much the cause of the leak being a problem but the work entailed in finding the leak. If you know what caused the leak it may help in finding its whereabouts. Since these ponds are generally punctured in some deliberate act of vandalism, then clues can be sought from punctures near the edge caused by sharp tools or knives, or from the landing spots of large rocks or bars launched from the bank.

Repair: If it isn't obvious where the leak is, this is when you wonder whether it was a good idea to have a pool and perhaps it may be easier to have a bog garden instead.

If, however, you are prepared to 'bite the bullet', it means a painstaking and careful excavation of the mud and detritus, peeling back the protective underlay on top of the liner and searching for the hole (but be prepared to find more than one). The repair to the liner is relatively straightforward with the relevant repair kit (see *Repair of Liners*, page 20). You will usually find it is necessary to discard the old underlay.

Vandal-Proofing Ponds

Whether the cause is accidental or intentional, when pond liner is punctured, it requires a lot of somebody's effort to repair it.

The usual 'last resort' for continual problems of this nature is to lay down a bed of concrete on top of the flexible liner in order to protect it. This has to be a minimum of 10cm (4in) thick, preferably with some reinforcement. Cracks can still appear in the concrete as it expands or contracts or as a result of land movement and the concrete shrinking.

Concrete is best engineered into place. The sides of a concrete pool need to be vibrated into place behind upright shuttering and the base needs to be flat and with a firm foundation.

liner turned up behind the stone

stone on a small footing

underlay

liner

30°

'Armater' bank stabilizing honeycomb or DIY version chicken wire laid on top of 25mm (2in) of concrete with a further 25mm (2in) laid on top of that.

The last resort...

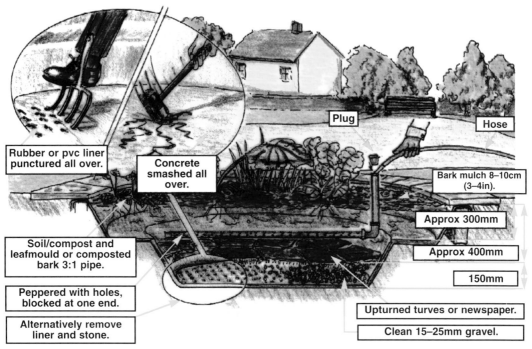

Plug

Hose

Rubber or pvc liner punctured all over.

Concrete smashed all over.

Bark mulch 8–10cm (3–4in).

Approx 300mm

Soil/compost and leafmould or composted bark 3:1 pipe.

Approx 400mm

150mm

Peppered with holes, blocked at one end.

Upturned turves or newspaper.

Alternatively remove liner and stone.

Clean 15–25mm gravel.

Turning your pool into a bog garden.

If you want to maintain your more 'organic' shape without the problems of getting wet concrete to stick to the incline of your pond, then Hampshire County Council have come up with an idea being tried by the British Trust for Conservation Volunteers (BTCV). A product called Armater is made from strips of polypropylene welded together to form a honeycomb layer. The cells of this honeycomb blanket are normally filled with soil so that it can be used for stabilising banks and soil on inclines. If, however, it is laid in the bottom of the pond on top of the liner, and the cells filled with concrete, it is perfect for holding together an armoured blanket of concrete over your liner, with enough flexibility to avoid unsightly cracks. It is expensive, but it is cheaper than paying for constant repairs.

DIY Vandal-Proofing on the Cheap

If your pond is small, and any vandalism will be somewhat casual, then a similar effect can be achieved with chicken wire sandwiched between two layers of cement. BTCV say in one of their Action Update releases that you must dig your pond 15cm (6in) deeper than you require and line the excavation with sand, carpets or underlay.

Then you can lay in your flexible liner followed by another layer of underlay or geotextile such as Terram. Lay a thick layer of cement on top of this.

Place chicken wire on top of the cement (this is much more easily said than done – carefully now). Lay more cement on top of the chicken wire. Leave the cement to go off.

I suggest that the pond is filled with water and left to stand for 24 hours to let the lime leach out of the cement.

Empty and repeat (fill, leave, empty).

After this, add a 10cm (4in) layer of subsoil that will provide a growing medium for your plants. The soil will also hide and protect the cement.

CHAPTER FIVE
BIOLOGICAL FILTERS

There are many effective ways of cleaning water. What concerns us here is the most effective way to remove algae, organic matter and the chemical nitrites and ammonia from pond water. This can be done almost as a single process so that conditions evolve which are self-sustaining with the minimum of maintenance. The key to this miracle is commonly called a **biological filter**.

Here is a process in which pond water is pumped through a medium that digests the rubbish in that water. A colony of bacteria uses the oxygen that is contained in the water to break down organic matter (the Nitrogen Cycle) through ammonia, to nitrites, to nitrates that get taken up by the plants. This is what would normally happen in the bottom of the pond. Therefore, theoretically, with a filter you can keep more fish in clearer, healthier water – or can you?

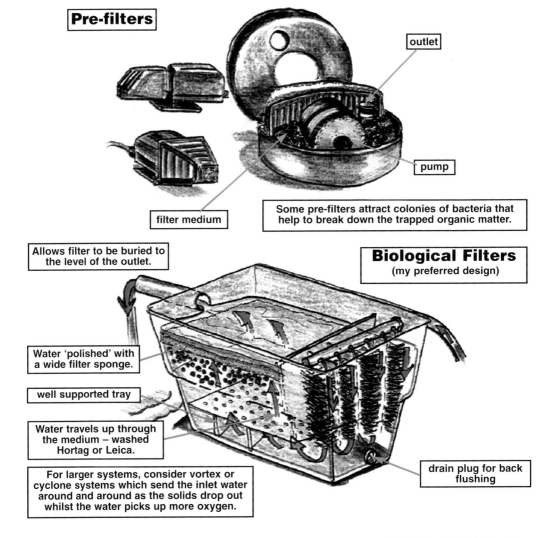

Pre-filters

outlet

pump

filter medium

Some pre-filters attract colonies of bacteria that help to break down the trapped organic matter.

Allows filter to be buried to the level of the outlet.

Biological Filters
(my preferred design)

Water 'polished' with a wide filter sponge.

well supported tray

Water travels up through the medium – washed Hortag or Leica.

For larger systems, consider vortex or cyclone systems which send the inlet water around and around as the solids drop out whilst the water picks up more oxygen.

drain plug for back flushing

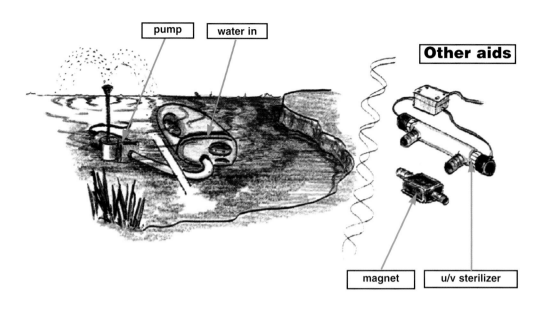

pump

water in

Other aids

magnet

u/v sterilizer

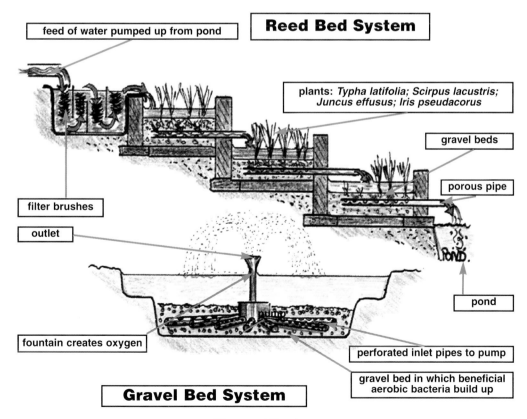

feed of water pumped up from pond

Reed Bed System

plants: *Typha latifolia; Scirpus lacustris; Juncus effusus; Iris pseudacorus*

gravel beds

porous pipe

filter brushes

outlet

pond

fountain creates oxygen

perforated inlet pipes to pump

gravel bed in which beneficial aerobic bacteria build up

Gravel Bed System

Filters and filtration

35

Pool Filters: Pros but Mostly Cons

The technology of biological pool filters has evolved to satisfy a demand by the pool enthusiast to see his fish at all times. The cause of him not seeing his fish is generally single-celled plants commonly known as algae. This, we imagine, is what the filter is designed to remove. Algae in water are quite natural and harmless, thriving in sunlight and lack of competition for the nutrients in the pond water. They don't harm the fish and, in fact, are a necessary link in the cycle of life in the pond. It is ironic that most filters do not remove many of those constituents in the water that are harmful.

Things that can be said against biological pool filters are:

1. They are expensive to buy from a retail outlet, but you could always make your own.
2. They do cover up what could be inadequate design in the pool specifications.
3. They are merely a stop gap in an overcrowded environment.
4. They cover up mismanagement of the pool environment with respect to overcrowding and also overfeeding.
5. They need to be running all the time – 24 hours a day – and this can create problems if you are going away for a long summer holiday.
6. Some of the detritus that is filtered out could be useful food in the pool, particularly for the baby fish and other 'beasties' of that bottom-dwelling world.
7. If you had not planned to have a filter, it may be awkward fitting it in. It may look unsightly. Many people have it running into an existing waterfall, but this takes some of the performance out of the pump and does not allow you to maintain the stream, repair it or even switch off the noise.
8. When you resort to a filter, you have become a confirmed fish keeper. I am not saying that there is anything wrong in this, but the water garden as a landscape feature, as another element or dimension in your garden, may be compromised as

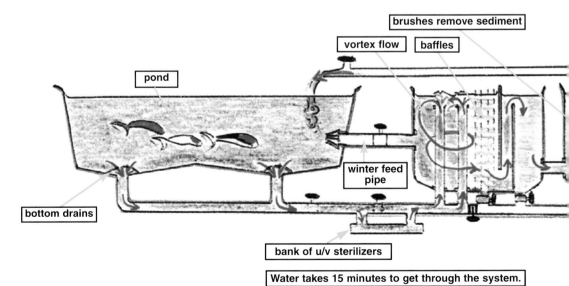

Large filter system using the principles of bottom drains and gravity feed.
Should be half the size of the pond/pool in surface area and able to process half the volume of the pool water every hour.

the passions of the hobby (which can become a way of life) take grip. The welfare of the fish becomes paramount to the detriment of the rest of the environment, ecologically and aesthetically. Filter systems emerge like power stations in the countryside; alarms and heron trip wires are like pylons carrying their hazardous cables thick and fast.

9.   The main reason why people purchase a filter is the presence of green water. If the filter is successful at making the water clear, beware of becoming complacent about whether the pond is a healthy environment.

Therefore ...

Before You Get a Filter

If you are colour blind, employ someone who isn't. The ability to recognise colour is an essential qualification for becoming 'the perfect pond detective'. Then, by using this and processes of deduction (if it isn't already obvious) you can make your own conclusions about the need for a filter and, subsequently, what may be wrong with the filter if you have any problems with it.

Also consider the type or style of your pond. There are different solutions to different problems in different pond environments. For instance, it would be silly to try to use a filter on a conservation/natural style of pool where the very definition of such a pond dictates the encouragement of the ecological and self-contained cycle within the pond. Besides which, many of these pools have soil bottoms which, apart from containing all the necessary bacteria, would soon clog up the pump and filter systems.

By the same token, it would be ludicrous to try to diminish the maulm or detritus at the bottom of the pond using a filter whilst at the same time using one of the clayey-type bacterial activators for the bottom of a pond. Horses for courses – so to speak.

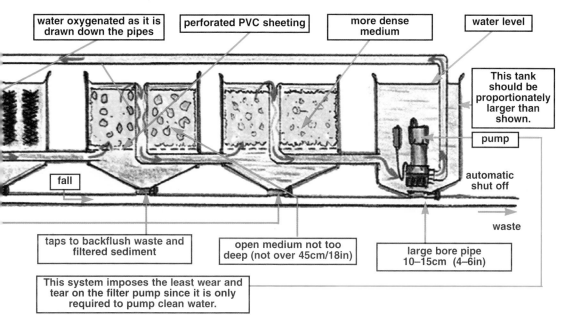

water oxygenated as it is drawn down the pipes

perforated PVC sheeting

more dense medium

water level

This tank should be proportionately larger than shown.

pump

fall

automatic shut off

waste

taps to backflush waste and filtered sediment

open medium not too deep (not over 45cm/18in)

large bore pipe 10–15cm (4–6in)

This system imposes the least wear and tear on the filter pump since it is only required to pump clean water.

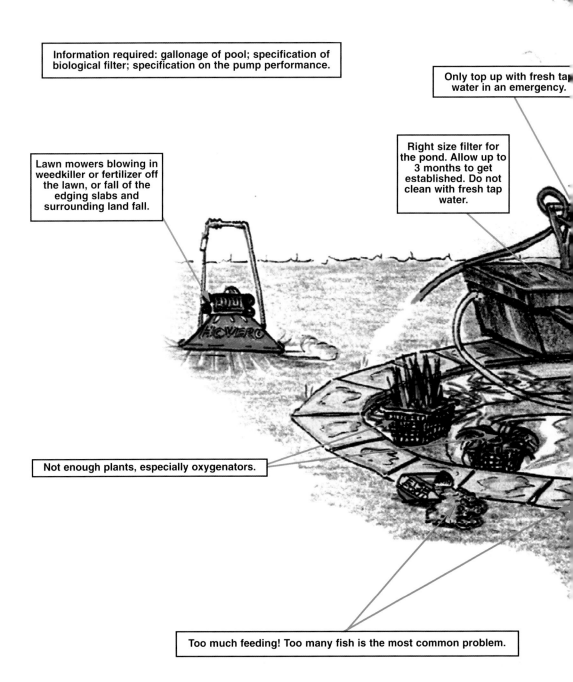

Information required: gallonage of pool; specification of biological filter; specification on the pump performance.

Only top up with fresh tap water in an emergency.

Right size filter for the pond. Allow up to 3 months to get established. Do not clean with fresh tap water.

Lawn mowers blowing in weedkiller or fertilizer off the lawn, or fall of the edging slabs and surrounding land fall.

Not enough plants, especially oxygenators.

Too much feeding! Too many fish is the most common problem.

Filtration vexation: problems that may hamper the efficiency of a biological filter.

hot humid weather

Is the filter operating 24 hours a day?

Keep the pond oxygenated. Run waterfalls and fountains.

Right size of pump for the filter?

Is the pump far enough away from the filter for complete recirculation of pool water? If it gets dirty quickly, raise it up from the bottom of the pool.

A dense pre-filter on the pump may be stopping the biological filter from doing its job properly. The pump must be capable of handling a certain amount of detritus.

'Make my day, unicellular Chlorophyceae!'

Different personalities produce different results when it comes to pond management. Some people like to cure problems with a sledge hammer type of approach. They might race into their nearest aquatic centre, fiercely grab the biggest bottle of 'Algalwallop' from the centre's shelves, burn off home and squirt the total contents (blithely double dosing) into the unsuspecting pond whilst screaming: 'Make my day, unicellular Chlorophyceae!' Others gently work their way towards a solution by trial and error, and often settle on a compromise.

(An algicide manufacturer once told me that the product he sold on the retail market was nearly half the strength necessary to provide the correct dosage at the dilution rates described on the bottle. He said that when they used to supply the stuff at the correct concentration to be effective for the correct quality of pool water, they were always getting complaints of dead plants and even deader fish. So now they dilute it, the customers are happily 'overdosing' and all they get is letters of approbation!)

The chemical approach may seem abhorrent to some people, but it might be argued that their problems could be cured by a single dose of algicide just to get the seesaw effect of the natural pond environment more consistently on the permanently clear side. However, Barley Straw, a natural 'pond start' chemical, a bag of Daphnia or even a dose of the water from a successfully clear pond can be enough to get the ball rolling (see *Perfect Pond Detective Book 1, Biological Balance*).

Another problem may be the pH of the water. A high pH encourages some forms of algae, in particular, blanket weed. It is possible to adjust the pH with chemicals or a plastic 'teabag' of peat pellets floating in the water. Stop fresh cement leaching lime into the pond by sealing it or treating it with Silglaze. Also stop topping up with high pH tap water.

Filters do not necessarily come into the equation straight away. If the problem is caused by those algae that cling together like the globular jelly types or grow in strands like the blanket weeds, then a filter by itself is not going to solve the problem.

Filter Problems

However, you have a filter and it has problems. The problems generally result from the original reason for resorting to a filter rearing its ugly head again. On the other hand, they might not be. A process of elimination must be followed; read on ...

Not working and has never been effective at keeping the water clear

Have you got the right parameters or filter specifications and is it set up right (see also *Rules and Parameters*)?

(a) The filter should be the right size for the pool and be capable of processing all the pool water. Do you know the gallonage of your pool? Pool gallonage = length x breadth x depth, all in feet x 6.25.

Originally, the filter formula was that the surface area should be one-third the surface area of the pool. Nowadays, with new filter mediums and stages of filtration combined in one unit, manufacturers claim we can get away with a lot less.

It should, however, be capable of processing the total volume of pool water once every two hours. Therefore, there must be a pump in the pool capable of delivering this to the filter. A filter that is suitable for a pool of 1000 gallons must have a submersible pump delivering 500 gallons every hour to the filter.

(b) In order to process all the water effectively the pump must be situated as far away from the filter as possible. This situation changes in the depths of winter for other reasons (see *Maintenance Schedule,* pages 12–15).
(c) The filter must be in operation 24 hours a day to be effective as a biological filter. What we have done in installing a filter is effectively to create a 'turbo-pool bottom'. If we are hoping to establish the bacteria that thrive on the bottom of the pools and digest dead algae and detritus, then we need to supply them with oxygen constantly. This is obtained from the persistent supply of water from the pool through the filter. This takes about a month to two months in good ambient weather conditions to really get established. It can be encouraged as well with special 'starter' chemicals or a small amount of filter medium borrowed from a neighbour's successful filter. Fish are also effective at priming the system, effectively fertilising the system with their excrement.
(d) Hopefully you have not been regularly topping up with fresh chlorinated tap water as this will provide minerals for the sustenance of algae and inhibit bacterial growth.
(e) If the pump to the filter has a pre-filter, that is, a sponge or a mesh over the inlet, it may be so fine that it is preventing enough of the waterborne matter from reaching the filter box itself and so stopping it from doing its job. If cleaning the pre-filter is a continual chore then get rid of it. If it is essential for the performance of the pump, then a more robust pump capable of delivering mucky water and suspended solids must be used.

The filter gets really dirty and clogs up really quickly – and is still not keeping the water clear

(a) If the filter has been recently installed, and is operating merely as a mechanical filter, it is bound to get really dirty. This will slow down the establishment of the correct bacteria, allowing pockets of anaerobic bacteria to get established that don't do any good if they become established too early and get hold of organic matter first. They can produce methane which is a poison to the pool environment.

When flushing out the filter to increase its efficiency, don't clean out too much of the muck and don't be tempted to use chlorinated tap water. This will wipe out the bacteria.

If the filter is really dirty you have probably found that the pump is also getting clogged up. Check that it has been delivering the correct quantity of water to the filter to make it effective. See how long it takes to fill up a 1 or 2 gallon bucket with water.

Particularly in the early establishment of the filter, you might find that there is too much muck on the bottom of the pond for the pump and filter to cope with, therefore it would be advisable to raise the pump up from the bottom temporarily.

(b) Is there enough oxygen in the pond to keep your filter alive? If the water does not seem to be half full of oxygenators then a fountain, waterfall or venturi is necessary to oxygenate the water supply to keep the filter going.

(c) Have you been using any chemical treatments? Neither algicide, pesticides or pond salt are of any benefit to filter systems and are detrimental even at prescribed doses.

The filter did work effectively for a while, but now gets really dirty and clogs up very quickly. It no longer keeps the water clear

(a) Is there enough oxygen in the pond to keep your filter alive (see above)?

(b) Have you been using any chemical treatments from algicides to pond salt (see above)?

(c) The reasons that may have galvanised you into fitting the filter system in the first place are still there, or have returned and are worse.

(d) Overcrowding of fish stock, stress and over-feeding are the commonest causes from a management point of view. These are not helped by inherent inadequacies of design, large, shallow areas where the water gets too warm, pollutants and water run off making their way into the pond. No shade and complex shapes do not help. Perhaps the filter's performance may be enhanced with extras such as u/v clarifiers or magnets (see below). These may buy you some more time before you really have to sort out the problem.

(e) It may be too cold, or at least the water may be. Below 10°C the filter is no longer operating biologically, as the bacteria in the medium do not break down organic matter below this temperature so the detritus just builds up. Circulating very cold water in a pond is probably not a very good idea anyway, particularly as the temperature drops towards 4°C. Therefore, it would be wise to clean the filter out thoroughly and put it to rest for the remainder of the winter.

Pool clear but ammonia or nitrite levels still high. Fish under stress and gasping at the surface

The filter may be operating efficiently, mechanically, but the effective breakdown of the chemicals in the water by the filter microbes is ineffective. This means that the bacteria are not established sufficiently to be effective for any of the above reasons, or:

(a) The filter is over-supplied with water and has not enough time to process it adequately.

(b) A sudden change or shock to the environment by outside environmental pressures, such as herons, weather, fertilisers and so on, causes sudden increases in metabolism in the fish which the filter cannot cope with initially.

Emergency treatment: Partial water change of between one third and one half of the water. Beware: if you partially empty the pool and the toxins are still building up in it, then there is a danger that they will concentrate even further.

Run fresh water in from a height so that oxygen can be pushed in and any chlorine in the water (if it is tap water) can be dissipated. Let the pool overflow. It is less of a shock to the fish. To estimate how much water you have actually changed, do a rough calculation on the gallonage per minute by squirting a hose into a 2-gallon bucket. From that you can extrapolate a time to fill half the gallonage of the pool. Remember to 'condition' the water, being on the generous side with the dosage.

A tonic dosage of salt will reduce the effects of the toxins but it won't do the filter much good. If you are using Zoolite as a filter medium, this will make the situation worse. (See also *Perfect Pond Detective Book 1: The Biological Balance: Unseen Water Problems – Ammonia and Nitrite*.)

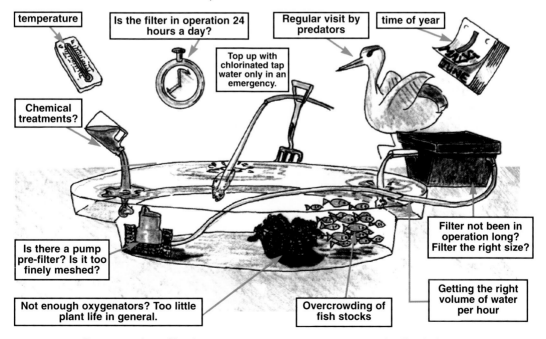

Reasons why a filtration system may not even start to work effectively.

Pool clear, nitrates high

Fertilisers and pollutants may be leaching in from the rockery or lawn surround.

Apart from outside environmental pressures, this may mean that, although the filter is working more than adequately even as a biological filter, you may need a further extension of it. The plant material in the pond is not large enough to be capable of using up the nitrates that emerge from the broken-down ammonia and nitrites. Therefore, you need to establish an extra process of filtration in which anaerobic bacteria break down the nitrates into nitrogen and oxygen. This would normally occur in the bottom of the pond but it may be so polished and pristine that a bug wouldn't be seen dead there!

The clarity is unsustainable in this situation as any algae will quickly take advantage of the nitrates and bloom. Blanket weed may, however, be the dominant algae and be taking advantage and helping sustain the water clarity.

Emergency treatment: Partial water change (see above, and also *Perfect Pond Detective Book 1: The Biological Balance – Nitrates*). Consider also a planted filter bed system, or anaerobic filtration.

Summary of Cures to Filter Problems

1   Patience is the first requirement in getting filters established. It can take anything from 1–3 months. 'Starters' from established efficient filters or proprietary pond start chemicals help.
2.   Carry out a water test even if it is just a pH test. This will give you a legion of clues as to the cause of the problem.
3.   Check filter specifications and pump performance. See how long the pump delivering water to the filter takes to fill a gallon bucket and work out how many gallons go through the filter every hour. If it is more than half the volume of the pond, then the filter is not getting a chance to filter the water. If it is a lot less, the same is true.
4.   Check that there have been no chemicals, soil or water making their way into the pond from outside. Is this a case of outside animal intrusion?
5.   Avoid cleaning out the filter with fresh tap water. Avoid regular 'top-ups' with the same.
6.   Less than 2in of fish per square foot in the pond? Any shade for the pool? Any oxygenation? Your filter needs all the help it can get during a long, hot summer.
7.   Check the u/v lamp. If you have not got one, then the next step might be – get one.

Once it established and working well, a quick visual check, along with a reassuring 'whiff' of the right blend of aromas, will be all that is necessary to confirm all is well within what is, effectively, the guts of the pond.

Ultra-Violet Lamp Water 'Clarifiers'

Mechanics

The water is pumped from the pond into the sterilizer unit where it passes over and around a glowing ultra-violet tube protected in a quartz sleeve. The effect of this is to damage the unicellular green algae to the extent that they die and are filtered out in the biological filter where they are digested by the colonies of aerobic bacteria. Some manufacturers claim that it makes them 'stick together' which makes them easier to trap in the filter medium.

For u/v lamps to be effective, they must be used in conjunction with a filter, or the dead algae simply return to the pond to rot on the bottom and become detritus for less benign bacteria to feed on or, at best, provide nutrition for the next generation of algae.

Ultra-violet lamps do not sterilise the water. They do very little to help produce pure water, but they do help us to see what is going on in the pond. That is, if the water is not cloudy because of mud being stirred up by the fish.

Problems

1. It is essential that the specifications of lamp (the wattage), match the requirements of the biological filter and the pump providing water for the system and in turn match the gallonage of the pond. For example, a 500-gallon pond = 250-gallon per hour pump to height of the filter, turning over the complete volume of the pond every 2 hours = 8 watt lamp. A 1000-gallon pond = 500 gallon per hour pump = 15 watt lamp.
2. Is the bulb still working? Never look at the working bulb itself, but see if there is a glow through the fittings at the ends or up through the hose tails. Don't dismantle the bulb unless it is not working. The design of these products, not to mention the facts that they have to cope with damp conditions and their connections are made of unstable alloys, causes deposits to build up, inhibiting the contact. The deposits very often 'weld' the connections together and it is virtually impossible to service the unit and take it apart without breaking the bulb. It helps to put it back together with a very thin smear of waterproof grease or vaseline on the connecting parts.
3. The lamp or tube needs to be changed every six months. Even if it is still working, its effectiveness is diminished in this time.
4. Beware of calcium deposits on the quartz sleeve which reduce the lamp's effectiveness. Many manufacturers recommend changing the sleeve regularly. This generally occurs anyway, since trying to dismantle the unit as it gets older without breaking any of the parts becomes increasingly difficult.

The lime deposits can be prevented by adding a specially-designed magnet on the inlet end of the water supply to the u/v clarifier.

Magnetic Treatment or 'Ionic Water Protection'

The precipitation of limescale on the inside of pipework and u/v silica quartz sleeves affects the performance of both pumps and filters. It is claimed that magnetic treatment of the water acts on the calcite minerals, affecting their ability to form scale. Therefore, used in conjunction with a UVC (see above), the performance is enhanced.

Of secondary benefit is the reduction of blanket weed. The ability to absorb these minerals seems to be essential to its growth. Once the magnet affects these minerals, the weed is unable to do this which, manufacturers claim, results in its 'virtual elimination'.

Why Have an Electrical Water Pump?

1. A fountain or waterfall can mean the difference between life and death for fish, particularly on a dark, stormy summer's evening when the plant life is not producing oxygen, or is even absorbing it.
2. What self-respecting fish-keeper does not have a filter so that he can see his fish at all times? And all filters need pumps.

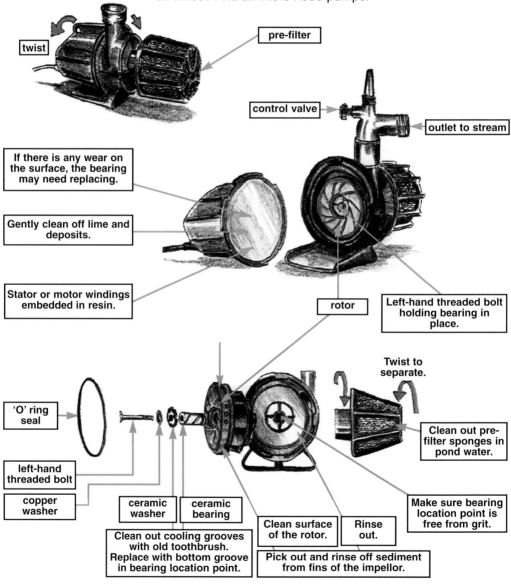

twist

pre-filter

control valve

outlet to stream

If there is any wear on the surface, the bearing may need replacing.

Gently clean off lime and deposits.

Stator or motor windings embedded in resin.

rotor

Left-hand threaded bolt holding bearing in place.

Twist to separate.

'O' ring seal

left-hand threaded bolt

copper washer

ceramic washer

ceramic bearing

Clean out cooling grooves with old toothbrush. Replace with bottom groove in bearing location point.

Clean surface of the rotor.

Pick out and rinse off sediment from fins of the impellor.

Rinse out.

Clean out pre-filter sponges in pond water.

Make sure bearing location point is free from grit.

Induction motor based on central heating pump design

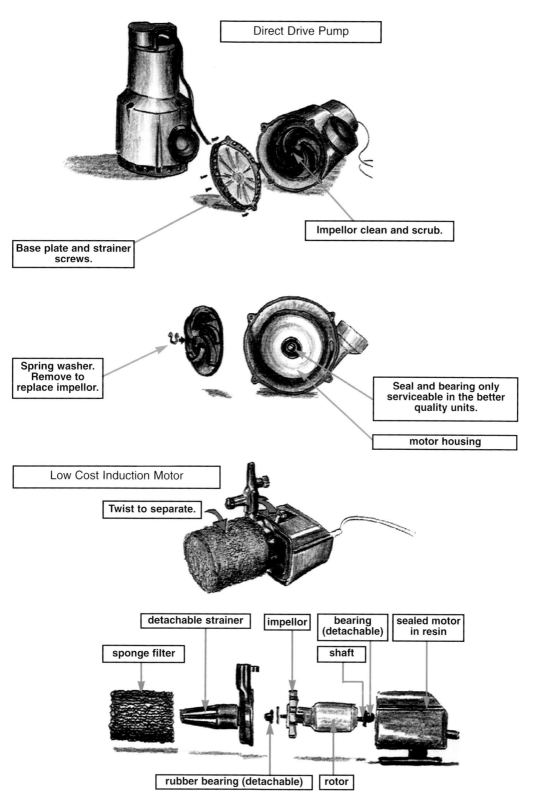

Direct Drive Pump

Impellor clean and scrub.

Base plate and strainer screws.

Spring washer. Remove to replace impellor.

Seal and bearing only serviceable in the better quality units.

motor housing

Low Cost Induction Motor

Twist to separate.

sponge filter

detachable strainer

impellor

bearing (detachable)

shaft

sealed motor in resin

rubber bearing (detachable)

rotor

In the world of industrial submersible pumps where murky water, sludge and solids are part of everyday life, engineers talk about direct drive pumps in terms of horsepower and kilowatts. These beasts munch up everything they take in and throw it out dozens of feet in the air. They can be taken apart right down to their basic components, worn parts replaced, and the pumps put back into service as good as new. But even for the smallest of these pumps that may be suitable for garden pools or fish filters, the manufacturers demand a premium more than double that which most consumers are prepared to pay.

In the cheaper world of the domestic market, many direct-drive pumps have started off on the drawing board as a cellar or a swimming pool/camping pump, or as an irrigation pump to be used in the occasional emergency. These are not continuously rated, but they do get sold to water gardeners as a waterfall pump or, even worse, as being suitable for filters. The power of the direct drive motors in these pumps makes them more suitable for a filter application with the extra torque and pushing power in

Before...

...and after.

particularly dirty water conditions. Bear in mind, however, that these are the conditions that put the dynamic seal and bearings in that much more jeopardy. Once again, the impellor design plays a significant part in this as well.

Impellor Design: Centrifuge or Not?

The design of impellor offers the direct drive and induction design of cheaper pumps a little more life expectancy.

Centrifugal Impellor Design

The water in which the impellor sits flows axially towards the impellor, is deflected by the disc of curved fins and flows out through the apertures between the vanes. Thus, the water undergoes a change of direction and is accelerated. This produces an increase in pressure at the pump outlet. On leaving the impellor the water may pass through a ring of fixed vanes which surrounds the impellor. Collectively, these vanes are called the diffuser. Because they are effectively widening passages, the velocity of the water is reduced and the kinetic energy of the water is converted into pressure energy. This conversion is completed in the volute of the pump, that is, the gradually-widening spiral casing. If the pump does not have this diffuser and the water passes directly from vanes to volute then it is not capable of a very high delivery head.

In essence, what is happening is that a vortex is created in the water, like water going down a plug hole, but instead this is being pushed out. The result is that any solids get pushed out too. As they rarely come into contact with weed and debris, the vanes and fins are less likely to get jammed and clogged up. As a result, centrifugal pumps are not self-priming and seem to need a good volume of water in the pump and up the pipework to get their steam up, so to speak.

Paddle Impellor Design

The alternative to the centrifugal pump vanes is chosen mainly for economy's sake. With the traditional little paddle impellor, a small, slow-running motor pushes the water along bit by bit. Although the torque of the motor may not be huge, the design of the electrics is such that probably it operates most efficiently with a bit of back pressure and at limited speed. It is quite possible that, if it were to operate for long periods with no head or back pressure, the life of the motor would be severely shortened.

The design of the flat impellor makes it particularly prone to becoming entangled in weed or debris, so it does need a very effective sponge filter. This again limits the performance and makes continual maintenance a chore. This fine filter would also make it useless in supplying water to an external filter system.

The main attraction of these pumps is that they are cheap to buy and those parts that are replaceable are generally inexpensive and easy to replace.

For a small fountain for a small pond, a tiny waterfall, or using the technology of 12 volt electricity from a transformer, these pumps are perfectly adequate and can give years of problem-free performance Remember, however, that cleanliness is next to godliness and keep an eye open for problems.

What Do You Need?

It may be that any problems you have with the pool stem from the wrong design or size of pump. You may be in the fortunate position of having yet to choose the right pump.

Most importantly, you must be aware of all your requirements before you buy. This will help your friendly aquatic dealer to know what he has got on offer that would suit you.

Is it for a fountain, waterfall or filter, or a combination of these?

With regard to a fountain, the plants have a problem. Lilies cannot abide being anywhere near splashing water, so leave plenty of room for both.

To stop the pump from spraying the total contents of the pool out over the lawn the one night you accidentally leave it on, position it at least the height of the spray clear from the edge of the pool.

Geyser type fountains or foaming jets have a more solid and less easily-blown column of water. They make very effective pool oxygenators, as well. They are easy to see and are non-clogging. However, they require a fairly substantial pump to keep them going.

If the pump is only for a waterfall, you don't really want any more than the total volume of the pool turning over every hour. The waterfall not only looks out of proportion but the pool has great difficulty in settling down and the plants have a hard time keeping on top of things. Allow 50–60 gallons per inch width of waterfall at the height/head you require.

If you want the pump to run a waterfall and a fountain, then reckon on the pump's performance at the waterfall being reduced by at least 20%.

Bearing everything in mind, go for a little more performance than you think you need. You can always restrict flow but you can never boost it, although direct drive pumps are less tolerant of too much restriction. Debris collecting in the pre-filter will soon dampen down the performance.

When it comes to plumbing in and siting the pump, remember again that the flora and fauna of the pool would prefer as little disturbance as possible from moving water. Therefore, site the pump as near as possible to the fountain or waterfall and as near to the surface (certainly raised from the bottom) to avoid as much turmoil as possible. This also reduces the pipework and, in turn, the loss of friction that professional pump suppliers regard as most important. For every foot of pipework, every fitting, bend or hose tail you are reducing your pump's performance by huge amounts. Therefore you must fit the widest possible hose that the pump will take and keep all fittings to a minimum (they are expensive, anyway), otherwise you might as well have bought a smaller pump.

Also, remember to see if the cable is long enough to reach from its designated station to the power supply connection. All modern pumps should be fitted with a minimum of 10 metres of cable which is adequate for most installations. If the pump needs to be situated in some vast lake then genuinely waterproof cable connectors can be obtained from electrical wholesalers at no little expense.

With pumps for filters you will want to turn over the complete volume of water in the pool once every two hours so it is probably necessary to situate the filter as far away as possible. Allow a loss of 7–10 gallons per hour in pump performance for every 10ft of maximum-bore piping. As well as taking this into account, the size of the pool and, therefore, the size of the filter will dictate the size of the pump required. For example, a 1000-gallon pool will need a filter capable of processing 500 gallons of water per hour and a pump capable of delivering that to the height of the filter.

I would not advocate running the outlet of a filter down a water course such as a stream, but just have the filter separately and unobtrusively discharging into the pool. In this way you can get maximum performance out of the filter and pump by having the filter situated more or less at pool level with the pump on the pool bottom in summer and halfway down in winter.

Summary of What to Look for in Filter Pump Design

1. A guarantee, and a minimum of one year continuously rated.
2. Pumps for filters need large inlet holes to take detritus to be filtered. Will it cope with suspended matter?
3. Pumps for filters should be powerful enough to get the maximum performance out of the filter which, in turn, should be capable of processing half the volume of the water in the pool every hour. Take the head into account. Take some gallon–litre conversion tables with you.
4. Centrifugal vanes on the impellor are less likely to get clogged.

5. If you are unsure about what you require, find someone who really knows what he is talking about. If you cannot, go somewhere else. If Mr Know-it-all really is busy, come back at a more convenient time when he is likely to be less harassed.

Remember

When costing for a pump, ask yourself where is the electrical power to the pump coming from, and how is it going to be fitted in? The cost of the bits and bobs, junction boxes, switches, plugs and cable can easily outstrip the cost of the pump. There is quality and rubbish in all this gear as well, and there is also the right way to do it. No short cuts, please.

RCDs

RCDs are residual circuit devices, rated at 30mA tripping. These are not MCBs (micro circuit breakers). They are *essential* for any electrical appliances outside, and you *must* follow the British Standards or IEE regulations for outdoor power installations, which is not cheap. Get professional help if you don't understand. See definition opposite.

Running Costs

With all the costs of installing your pump, you might feel that the running costs are pretty insignificant in comparison. It is worth checking to see whether if a particular pump is more expensive, it has lower running costs for the same performance. As probably it is going to be run non-stop, it might tip the balance towards that better-quality pump.

What makes one pump more expensive than another, and another cheaper to run for the same amount of power input to power output, is inherent in the design. It is a mistake to consider 'wattage' as an indication of the 'strength' of a motor. In proportion to its performance, it is a guide to its efficiency.

I would add to this that whatever the temptation, buy locally, even if it is a tiny bit more expensive. If something does go wrong within the pump, you can take it back.

Technical Terms and Symbols on Pumps and their Boxes

Amperes, or current of electricity, is the rate of flow of an electric charge through a particular conductor at a given instant.

Current is calculated by dividing the voltage (volts) by the resistance of the circuit (measured in ohms).

Ohm is a unit of electrical resistance.

Bar is a unit of pressure equal to 10m = water column (1 bar = 14.5 psi, ie, pounds per square inch).

Flow rate defines the volume of water in a certain period, for instance, l/s (litres per second), l/m (litres per minute), m^3/h (cubic metres per hour ($1m^3/h = 16.671/min$)). By the way, 1000 litres per hour = 225 gallons per hour (gph).

Pump performance curves show the output from a pump in litres, gallons or cubic metres against a head pressure height of a column of water in metres, feet or bars (1 bar = 10 metre water column). They are usually self-explanatory, but can be misleading because you should not expect any worthwhile performance by operating the pump near the top of its potential head.

Rated voltage is the voltage supply for which the pump is suitable. In Europe the standard voltage is 220/50hz, in the British Isles 230/50hz, and in the USA 110/60hz. Electrical equipment must be suitable for a voltage variation of 10% over or 6% under the available supply.

RCDs, or residual circuit devices, provide protection against a build-up of earth faults if they reach a predetermined level. This is generally expressed in mA – these should be 30mA or less. Apart from being sensitive to small fault currents to earth via high resistance paths that could cause a fire, they will detect small currents to earth via the human body and will disconnect the voltage hopefully in 10–30 milliseconds, thus preventing electrocution.

A *kilowatt* is 1000 watts. If we run an appliance or machine that uses 1000 watts for one hour, in Great Britain we use one 'unit' of electricity. This is the unit by which our electricity bill is measured, the kilowatt hour (kWh).

Troubleshooting Pump Problems

If the waterfall, fountain or filter does not actually work physically when switched on:

1. Check the trip switch on the RCD. If this refuses to stay on, it is not necessarily a cause for concern, since it is extremely sensitive and can be affected by dampness and humidity building up in connections.

Cure: Disconnect the pump and any other items on the circuit and work through them by a process of elimination. If, when the pump is connected, it trips the RCD and the connectors or plugs are bone dry inside and out (and connected properly), then the pump is faulty. Test it for continuity if you have an electrical meter and take it back to the shop from where you got it to exchange for another one.

2. If the trip stays on and there is no action from the pump, switch it off and remove it from the pond.

Clues: If it is covered in filth and rubbish it could be starved of water. Clean off the worst from around the intakes. Rinse out the pre-filter if there is one. Step back and switch it on again **very briefly**. If it bursts into life the job is done. If it seems merely to 'hum' thoughtfully, then the impellor could be jammed. This means removing the housing around the impellor, which is generally straightforward and at most requires the use of a screw driver to remove half a dozen screws. Many modern designs just clip together.

After exposing the impellor, carefully clean the fins and any passageways for the water. Over time, there is always a build-up of sediment in various nooks and crannies. It is a good idea to make this a routine task at a minimum of six-monthly intervals.

If it is a direct drive pump with the impellor attached to the main shaft running through the motor, try turning its power supply on very briefly before you put it back together. The impellor should spin into life and run very quietly. If it rattles, the impellor has come adrift from the shaft, or the bearings are worn. This is repairable on the better and, generally, more expensive pumps. The amount of free play will confirm the problem.

3. With both the direct drive pump and the induction design, try running them in clean water detached from what they would normally run, just below the surface of the water, to see if there is any pressure from any water pushed through. This will show whether the motor is old and tired or completely broken down.

If it is an induction motor, then in any case it will only run when the unit is put together. However, any problems with the impellor will be obvious when you service it. The bearings may be at fault if it runs freely when dismantled and jams when it is put back together. Slightly worn bearings are more of a problem in some designs:

(a) If any seals or 'O' rings are worn or left out.
(b) If on the surface of the motor housing there is a build-up of lime from hard water.
(c) The motor housing plate is worn or pitted by grit in the water getting through because of a missing pre-filter.
(d) If the unit has been left out in the sun or has been working without water running through it for some length of time, the motor may have over-heated and the facing plate has warped.
(e) The facing plate or housing may not have been perfectly smooth in the first place and, as soon as the bearing 'runs in', after a few hours the pump seizes.

Another problem that can arise in the early days of running an induction pump is if the unit has ceramic bearings. Such bearings must be made to exact specifications. Because they are so hard wearing, any tiny 'high spots' refuse to wear away, or restrictions in lubrication channels soon make themselves a nuisance and the unit seizes. The pump itself might 'unseize' as the unit cools down, which makes the situation doubly annoying when you take it back and it performs quite adequately on the retailer's counter.

Cures: For direct drive pumps, the immediate remedy should make itself plain, but to prevent a recurrence of the problem, consider adding a pre-filter to the pump. Certainly avoid running it right on the bottom of the pool. Raise it up on a block.

Depending on the quality, an induction pump is repairable. Certainly new impellors, rotors, seals and bearings are often available.

4. If the pump seems to run satisfactorily in clean water there may be a blockage in the pipework.

(a) Waterfalls and streams: check there is a clear outlet. Outlets underwater suck down pebbles and muck that siphons back to the pump when you turn it off.

(b) In narrow pipework, especially that exposed to sunlight when going to ornaments, great gobbets of algae build up like cholesterol in arteries and come away and block the pipe with thromboid blobs.

(c) Some pumps, particularly those that have a centrifugal design of impellor, need a certain amount of water in the pipework to get the centrifugal effect going. In this case the pump should be sitting in deeper water so that more pipework sits below the surface. Alternatively, you can try turning the pump off and then on a couple of times. This sometimes helps the momentum.

(d) Long lengths of pipe sometimes collect air bubbles or 'airlocks' as some but not all of the water drains back to the pond through the pump. When the pump is turned on, these airlocks act as buffers against the water being pushed up from the pump. These can effectively take the momentum out of quite powerful pumps. Try switching the pump off and on slowly several times to bash the bubbles through.

Handy Hint

When removing the pump for servicing or examination, try to avoid pulling it out by the cable. Also make sure it is switched off. If the problem is an electrical 'leakage', then you will be the first to find out.

CHAPTER SEVEN
COMMON CHEMICALS

Whilst I do not approve of the random use of chemicals in the pond environment, there are cases, particularly if the pond is fairly small, where, if the balance of the pond goes slightly out of kilter or pressure has been put on it from the outside world by accidents or weather, a little judicious medication may get things settled again *(status quo ante bellum)*.

Adding any chemicals to the pond *must* be done accurately and precisely according to the manufacturer's instructions. You have no-one else to blame if they don't work.

Malachite Green and Formalin

General
- Used for parasite treatments. Can be used together. You must use the correct dosage; too little and the parasites become immune, too much, and you kill off the bacterial activity in the pond.
- Keep the pond aerated.
- Stop feeding the fish.
- Turn off the filter during application. This can be started up again one hour after application.
- Do not use below 50°F.
- Do not repeat dosage within 7–10 days.
- Mixtures: 3.3g of solid Malachite Green in one litre of Formalin.
- Dosage: 1.5ml of mixture to 100l/17.6gal continuously until cured.

Malachite Green
- Used against fungus, slime disease, white spot and other parasites such as skin flukes. Use in conjunction with either common salt or Formalin, not both.
- Breaks down in sunlight. Administer in the evening and use as fresh a source as possible.
- If using directly onto wounds, use only on very small ones. Neat malachite can lead to liver disorders. Also it can burn the skin of the fish in a way that may take years to heal properly.
- Can cause problems in very hard water areas.
- Dosage: 2ml per 100 litres bath for 30 mins.
  1ml per 100 litres pool continuously until cured. Repeat after 7 days.

Formalin
Never use Formalin in conjunction with salt. Unless the pond is cleaned out after a salt treatment it will always be there. Formalin is probably the most poisonous of these chemicals to your pond ecosystem and your filter. It is rarely used alone. Generally, it is best used in conjunction with Malachite Green as above.

Potassium Permanganate
- Can be used to clear algae from water but also as a treatment for many parasites.
- Don't use in conjunction with salt.
- Stop feeding the fish.

- One quarter of a teaspoon mixed in one gallon for every 200 gallons in the pool. Distribute the mixture over as much the surface of the pool as possible. (This is an old timer's recipe – *not* the sort that would become an EU legislated standard!)

Salt

- Long-term treatment or tonic. Fish can be allowed to feed during treatment.
- Effective against bacterial disease.
- Monitor concentration with specific gravity unit.
- A 3–10 minute bath may be better than a pond dose.
- For parasites and cloudy eye as it increases mucous flow: 3kg per 100 litres pool bath for 10 minutes.
  Tonic to aid recovery from various diseases and ulcers: 1kg per 100 litres pool for 1–2 weeks.
  As a tonic and to reduce effect of ammonia and nitrites: 300g per 100 litres continuous until cured.

Pool Conditioner

Safely removes chlorine and other halogens, heavy metals and other toxic elements commonly found in fresh tap water. Pool conditioner tends to contain special protective colloids which mimic the natural mucous secretions of the fish. This helps to reduce the effect of shock or stress on fish, and can be used as a tonic for fish newly introduced to the pond environment.

Proprietary Remedies

A host of proprietary remedies is available that are mainly cocktails of the above but are probably safer and easier to use. Also, as long as you follow the instructions precisely, they may be more effective.

Other Chemicals

Other chemicals may include Pond Start preparations designed to start up the biological activity in the filter and pond after a cleaning or a long, hard winter. At the same time, they provide protective colloids that help to supplement the fishes' mucous membranes, helping them through a traumatic period.

Some chemical manufacturers claim that the biological activity may stimulate the bacterial activity enough to digest much of the muck on the bottom of the pond. It works for some.

BIBLIOGRAPHY
Bibliography

Every home with a pond should have *The Observers' Book of Pond Life* by John Clegg. First published by Warne in 1956.

The Completely Illustrated Guide to Koi for your Pond by Dr. Herbert Axelrod , Balon, Hoffman, Rothbard and Wohlfarth. TFH Publications Inc.

Brookes, Alan and Agate, Elizabeth, *Waterways and Wetlands*, (BTCV) Heritage, Bill, *Ponds and Water Gardens*, Blandford. This is *the* man in the field. Perry, Frances, Water Gardens. She is *the* lady.

You should also subscribe to the magazines available from your newsagent:
The Water Gardener Magazine, Practical Fishkeeping and *Aquarist and Pond Keeper*, from which you will receive much useful information, handy hints and tips.

CONVERSION TABLES

Length

1 inch	=	25.4 millimetres
1 inch	=	2.54 centimetres
1 foot	=	30.5 centimetres
1 foot	=	0.305 metres
1 yard	=	0.914 metres
1 mile	=	0.609 kilometres

1 millimetre	=	0.0394 inches
1 centimetre	=	0.394 inches
1 metre	=	39.4 inches
1 metre	=	3.28 feet
1 metre	=	1.09 yards
kilometre	=	0.621 miles

Weight

1 ounce	=	28.3 grams
1 pound	=	454 grams
1 pound	=	0.454 kilograms
1 ton	=	1.02 metric tonnes

1 gram	=	0.035 ounces
1 kilogram	=	2.2 pounds
1 metric tonne	=	2200 pounds
1 metric tonne	=	0.984 tons

Capacity

1 fluid ounce	=	28.4 millilitres
1 pint	=	0.568 litres
1 UK gallon	=	4.55 litres
1 UK gallon	=	1.2 US gallons

1 millilitre	=	0.035 fluid ounces
1 litre	=	1.76 pints
1 litre	=	0.22 UK gallons
1 US gallon	=	0.833 UK gallons

Area

1 sq in	=	6.45 sq centimetres
1 sq foot	=	929 sq centimetres
1 sq foot	=	0.093 sq metres
1 sq yard	=	0.836 sq metres
1 acre	=	0.405 hectares
1 sq mile	=	259 hectares
1 sq mile	=	2.59 sq kilometres

1 sq centimetre	=	0.155 sq inches
1 sq metre	=	10.76 sq feet
1 sq metre	=	1.2 sq yard
1 hectare	=	2.47 acres
1 sq kilometre	=	247 acres
1 sq kilometre	=	0.386 sq miles

Volume

1 cu inch	=	16.4 cu centimetres
1 cu foot	=	0.028 cu metres
1 cu yard	=	0.765 cu metres

1 cu centimetre	=	0.061 cu inches
1 cu metre	=	35.3 cu feet
1 cu metre	=	1.31 cu yards

Abbreviations

centimetre(s)	=	cm
foot, feet	=	ft
gram(s)	=	g
inch(es)	=	in
kilogram(s)	=	kg
metre(s)	=	m
millimetre(s)	=	mm
ounce(s)	=	oz
pound(s)	=	lb
litre(s)	=	l

INDEX

A

algae 13, 18, 36, 41
ampere 54
anaerobic bacteria 42, 44
Armater 33
area 6
armoured cable 9
autumn 13, 30

B

bacteria 42
bar 54
barley straw 40
biological balance 6
biological filter 22, 35–45
boggy area 6

C

capillary action 19, 20
cement 29, 33
centrifugal motor 48, 51
chemicals 18, 40, 42, 58–59
clay pond 21
concrete 18, 19, 20–21, 32
conditioner 59
conservation pond 30, 37
construction 7, 29
current 54

D

design 7
direct drive pumps 49–50, 55, 56, 57

E

electrics 9–10, 13, 20
emergency 16
ensured water level 30
evaporation 18, 23
external pump 48

F

fibreglass 21, 28
filters 10–11, 13, 65, 34–35, 41, 42
  leaks 22, 24–25

reasons for 36–37
  problems 43
filter medium 41, 43
filter pump 41
fish 36, 43
fittings 23
flow rates 54
Formalin 58
fountains 17, 18, 52
  leaks 23

G

gallonage 41, 43
green water 18, 37

H

hairline cracks 21
herons 19

I

impellor 48, 51–52, 55
induction drive 49, 56
ionic water protection 45

K

kilowatt 55

L

leaks 14, 33
liner 6, 7, 17, 18–20, 28, 29, 31

M

magnet 42, 45
maintenance 12
Malachite Green 58
marginal planting 7, 8, 13, 31
materials 7, 18, 20, 23
methane 42

N

National Standards 10, 54
nitrates 34
Nitrogen Cycle 34

O

ohm 54
outdoor circuit 10
oxygenators 11, 23, 42

P

paddle impellor design 52
paint 21
pea gravel 29
pH 40
planning 6
Potassium Permanganate 58–59
prefiller 34, 41, 55
preformed plastic 28
proprietary remedies 59
puddled ponds 21, 30
puddling 31
pump performance curve 54
pumps 10, 12, 13, 26, 30, 41, 46–57

Q

quartz sleeve 45

R

rated voltage 55
reed bed system 35
reeds and rushes 31
residual circuit devices (RCDs) 54, 55

S

salt 43, 59
sealants 18
seepage 29
shape of pond 6
siphoning 16, 19, 20, 26, 28
site. 6
size 6
soil 19, 31
sponge filter 52
spring 12
stonework 19, 29
stream 7, 8
submersible pump 48
sun 6, 7, 21
surface render 21

T

3-phase electricity 9
tap water 40, 41, 43
temperature 42
top-up devices 30
trees 6
tubing 13

U

ultra-violet light 7, 10, 42, 44
underlay 19

V

varnish 21
vandals 32–33

W

water
  clarity 11
  density 12
  level 30
  loss 14–33
waterfall 7, 8, 16, 26, 27–30, 52
water level detection device 30
water table 6, 20
weep holes 30
wick effect 18
wild life 19
wind 6, 23
winter 12, 41, 42